Thirteen friends purchase bus tickets to New Orleans, Louisiana. They plan to reach that city on May 17 to help celebrate the seventh anniversary of the U.S. Supreme Court's *Brown v. Board of Education* decision. They are men and women, young and old, black and white. They are people with a plan. They chat quietly, nervously, excitedly. They are prepared for the unexpected.

LARRY DANE BRIMNER

CALKINS CREEK
AN IMPRINT OF HIGHLIGHTS
Honesdale, Pennsylvania

TWELVE DAYS IN MAY

FREEDOM RIDE 1961

For Cindy Clevenger and
Kathleen Krull, with thanks

For information about permission to reproduce
selections from this book,
please contact permissions@highlights.com.

Calkins Creek
An Imprint of Highlights
815 Church Street
Honesdale, Pennsylvania 18431
Printed in China

ISBN: 978-1-62979-586-7 (hc) • 978-1-62979-917-9 (e-book)

Library of Congress Control Number: 2017937780

First edition

10 9 8 7 6 5 4 3 2 1

Designed by Barbara Grzeslo
Titles set in Impact
Text set in Courier Bold and Adobe Caslon

LANDMARK EVENTS BEFORE THE TWELVE DAYS IN MAY

Plessy v. Ferguson (1896)

On June 7, 1892, Homer Plessy, a light-complexioned black man, deliberately sat in the white-only car of the East Louisiana Railroad. He identified himself as Negro and was arrested for violating Louisiana's Separate Car Act, passed in 1890. The act segregated railroad passengers by race. Plessy wanted to test the law, and his case eventually reached the U.S. Supreme Court. The court ruled that separate facilities for blacks and whites were constitutional as long as they were equal. This separate-but-equal doctrine eventually was applied to all areas of life—restaurants, theaters, schools, waiting rooms, restrooms, and even drinking fountains. The facilities for blacks were never equal.

Morgan v. Commonwealth of Virginia (1946)

Irene Morgan, a black woman, boarded a bus going from Virginia to Baltimore, Maryland. She was ordered to sit in the back of the bus. She objected, saying the laws and the Constitution of the United States, not Virginia segregation laws, applied since the bus was an interstate bus (one that crossed state boundaries). She was arrested and fined $10, but Morgan

Separate-but-equal was the law of the land following the U.S. Supreme Court's *Plessy* decision, but accommodations for blacks were always inferior, never equal.

took her case to the Supreme Court. The court ruled in Morgan's favor. The laws of one state cannot extend beyond its borders. To avoid a patchwork of regulations in which some states racially segregated passengers and others did not, the court saw a need for a single, uniform rule for interstate passengers. Segregated seating on interstate buses was declared unconstitutional, but the court's ruling did not apply to buses traveling only within a state.

Brown v. Board of Education (1954)

In 1954, a large portion of the United States had segregated schools as a result of the *Plessy* decision. A black third-grader in Topeka, Kansas, named Linda Brown would help bring an end to the separate-but-equal doctrine established in *Plessy*. Linda could not attend the white-only school just six blocks from her house. She had to catch a bus to attend a segregated school a mile away. Oliver Brown, Linda's father, filed a lawsuit. But it was later combined with other cases making their way to the Supreme Court. The Browns and other plaintiffs claimed that racially segregated schools violated the Equal Protection Clause of the Fourteenth Amendment to the Constitution. The Equal Protection

At their black-only school, children gather to warm themselves
around a stove in their classroom. Black youngsters relied
on tattered, used textbooks and supplies handed down from

In 1958, Bruce Boynton, a black Howard University law student, boarded a bus in Washington, D.C., bound for Montgomery, Alabama. In Richmond, Virginia, the bus stopped briefly so passengers could eat. Boynton went into the terminal restaurant and sat in the white-only section. When told to move, he refused, was arrested, and fined $10. He took his case to the Supreme Court. The *Morgan* decision had ruled that racial segregation in interstate transportation was unconstitutional. Now in *Boynton*, the court extended its ruling, declaring that segregation among interstate passengers at bus station facilities—restaurants, lunch counters, waiting rooms, and restrooms—also violated the law.

Young students, black and white, from six Texas schools
protest segregation in 1949.

THE SIT-INS

In February 1960, four black students from North Carolina Agricultural and Technical State University took seats at the local Woolworth's white-only lunch counter in Greensboro, North Carolina. They politely ordered coffee, but they were refused service and asked to leave. When they told their classmates about what had happened, the local protest grew in size. Within two months, more than seventy thousand young people—black and white—in fourteen states were conducting sit-in campaigns. The protests eventually spread throughout the United States wherever discrimination was practiced.

The Greensboro, NC, sit-ins began when David Richmond,
Franklin McCain, Ezell Blair Jr. (known now as Jibreel Khazan),
and Joseph McNeil sat down on February 1, 1960, at
Woolworth's white-only lunch counter and waited for service.
(Press photographers were not allowed into the store the first
day of the demonstration.) On the second day of the peaceful
protest, McNeil (seated, from left) and McCain are joined by
Billy Smith and Clarence Henderson, and more than a dozen
others as the sit-in movement grew.

MAY 1961

SUNDAY	MONDAY	TUESDAY	WEDNESDAY
	1	2	3
7	8	9	10
14 MOTHER'S DAY	15	16	17
21	22	23	24
28	29 MEMORIAL DAY	30	31

THURSDAY	FRIDAY	SATURDAY
4	5	6
11	12	13
18	19	20
25	26	27

TWELVE DAYS IN MAY
FREEDOM RIDE 1961

MAY 4

A blue-and-silver bus with a sleek dog painted on its side waits at the Greyhound terminal in Washington, D.C. Across the street at the Continental Trailways station, one of that company's red-and-cream buses stands idle also, awaiting passengers. It is Thursday.

Five of the original thirteen Freedom Riders study a map of the route they plan to take from Washington, D.C., to New Orleans, Louisiana. They are (left to right): Edward Blankenheim, James Farmer, Genevieve Hughes, the Reverend Benjamin Cox, and Henry "Hank" Thomas.

Thirteen friends purchase bus tickets to New Orleans, Louisiana. They plan to reach that city on May 17 to help celebrate the seventh anniversary of the U.S. Supreme Court's *Brown v. Board of Education* decision. They are men and women, young and old, black and white. They are people with a plan. They chat quietly, nervously, excitedly. They are prepared for the unexpected.

Each has a small carry-on "bag containing a toothbrush, toothpaste, and an inspiring book or two" just in case the unexpected includes jail. Twenty-one-year-old John Lewis, one of the riders, has three books in his bag: "one by [Catholic philosopher] Thomas Merton, another about Gandhi and the Bible."

The hour arrives.

They give their tickets to the drivers and board the buses—six on the Greyhound, seven on the Trailways. "Freedom Ride 1961" is underway. It is a ride that will shock a nation, and the world.

WHO'S ON THE BUSES?

JAMES FARMER, 41 (BLACK): The organizer and leader of Freedom Ride 1961.

JAMES PECK, 46 (WHITE): A lifelong pacifist and longtime activist in the civil rights movement. **GENEVIEVE HUGHES, 28 (WHITE):** From the southern state of Maryland. Volunteers for Freedom Ride 1961 because she believes the nation needs to realize that not all Southerners think alike. One of two women originally chosen for the ride. **JOSEPH "JOE" P. PERKINS JR., 27 (BLACK):** Active in the Ann Arbor Direct Action Committee, a nonviolent student-run civil rights group dedicated to integration at the University of Michigan. **WALTER BERGMAN, 61 (WHITE):** The oldest Freedom Rider. A retired school administrator and part-time professor from Michigan. **FRANCES BERGMAN, 57 (WHITE):** The second-oldest Freedom Rider. A former elementary-school teacher and assistant principal. **ALBERT SMITH BIGELOW, 55 (WHITE):** A Harvard graduate, retired naval officer, and an architect. **JIMMY MCDONALD, 29 (BLACK):** A folk singer from New York City. **EDWARD "ED" BLANKENHEIM, 27 (WHITE):** A part-time chemistry student at the University of Arizona, Tucson, and Korean War veteran. **HENRY "HANK" THOMAS, 19 (BLACK):** A Howard University student and volunteer at the Nonviolent Action Group, a student-run organization that campaigns against racial segregation through sit-ins and other demonstrations.

CHARLES PERSON, 18 (BLACK): The youngest Freedom Rider and a freshman at Atlanta's Morehouse College. **BENJAMIN ELTON COX, 29 (BLACK):** A pastor of a church in High Point, North Carolina, where he has earned a reputation for spearheading school desegregation efforts. **JOHN LEWIS, 21 (BLACK):** A theology student in Tennessee. Wants to be a preacher and is involved in Nashville's student activist movement.

The thirteen Freedom Riders take their seats.
All volunteers, they have been recruited by ride
leader James Farmer of the Congress of Racial
Equality (CORE), a mixed-race civil rights group,
for their experience fighting discrimination and their
willingness to remain nonviolent, no matter what.
They sit where they choose. This is the plan. It is also
the law of the United States. But in the South, people
don't follow the law. In the South, it is blacks to the
back, whites only at the front. Segregation. Keep the
races apart. Keep them separate.

They call it Jim Crow.

The thirteen riders do not believe in Jim Crow.

James Farmer (seated), leader of the Freedom Ride and
director of the Congress of Racial Equality, integrates a white-
only lunch counter. (The gentleman standing next to Farmer
is unidentified.)

At first, nobody pays attention to the thirteen riders on this "sit-in on wheels." But there is more to their plan than riding the buses and sitting where they choose. When the Greyhound makes its first stop at the bus terminal in Fredericksburg, Virginia, some fifty miles south of Washington, the riders see the signs of the South, the Jim Crow signs:

WHITE
COLORED

These are posted above restroom doors.
White here. Colored there.
Segregation.
The Supreme Court says the signs should welcome all.
The Freedom Riders put another part of their plan into action. They follow the law of the United States, not the Jim Crow signs of the South.

Buses and trains were the main ways to travel before automobile ownership became commonplace in the United States. Despite the Supreme Court's *Morgan* and *Boynton* rulings that prohibited segregated seating and facilities serving interstate passengers, the South generally ignored these decisions and the federal government failed to enforce them.

The youngest rider, eighteen-year-old Charles Person, enters the white-only restroom. Later, he orders a drink at the white-only lunch counter.

James Peck chooses to use the colored-only restroom.

PERSON IS BLACK. PECK IS WHITE.

The service at the lunch counter is pleasant. Nobody says anything about the two Freedom Riders ignoring the signs of the South.

Before long, the Freedom Riders stop in Richmond, Virginia. The riders do not expect a warm welcome. At one time, Richmond was the capital of the Confederate States of America—THE SOUTH. The local leader of the National Association for the Advancement of Colored People (NAACP) warns the group's followers to avoid the riders, avoid trouble.

There is no trouble. The riders receive only "a few cold stares." The segregation signs are gone from Richmond's bus terminals. Despite the signs' absence, people still tend to follow the Jim Crow customs of the South: blacks confining themselves to the waiting room, restroom, and lunch counter that have always been set aside for them, and most whites expecting this observance of tradition.

MAY 5

On Friday, the same day astronaut Alan B. Shepard becomes the first American in space, the Freedom Riders leave their buses to spend the night in Petersburg, Virginia. A little over twenty-three miles south of Richmond, Petersburg desegregated its bus terminals in August 1960 after a series of nonviolent lunch-counter sit-ins.

Upon splashing down safely in his space capsule, Shepard says, "It's a beautiful day."

It *is* a beautiful day.

Men and women, young and old, black and white—together—in Petersburg.

Although Petersburg, Virginia, desegregated its bus terminals in 1960, this was the exception rather than the rule in the South. When Freedom Ride 1961 ended in Birmingham, Alabama, on May 15, new waves of riders picked up the cause. Here, unidentified Freedom Riders successfully integrate the bus terminal in Montgomery, Alabama, on May 28, 1961.

MAY 6

On Saturday, the Freedom Ride buses are still rolling through Virginia. That evening in Lynchburg, the thirteen split up to visit churches. They explain their purpose is to demonstrate that the law of the land is not being followed everywhere in these United States. Most are politely received. But at Court Street Baptist Church, a black congregation, where Ben Cox is the chosen speaker, the minister gives him a warning: "If God had wanted us to sit in the front of the bus, he would have put us there." Cox and the other Freedom Riders are speechless.

In Danville, Virginia, a black waiter refuses to serve Ed Blankenheim at the combined Greyhound-Trailways station. The white Freedom Rider sits at the colored-only lunch counter.

The waiter's white boss has promised to fire him if he serves any Freedom Rider who ignores the signs of the South. Blankenheim is patient, polite, but he is refused.

After a wait, he returns to his bus.

When the Trailways bus arrives at the Danville terminal a short while later, James Peck, Genevieve Hughes, and Walter Bergman, all white, also sit at the colored-only counter. At first, the trio is refused service, but they tell the station manager about the *Boynton* decision. This time the station manager relents.

INTEGRATION.

It is a small step toward victory for the Freedom Riders. Peacefully, nonviolently, they have integrated the Danville bus station by explaining the law of the land.

Ed Blankenheim (left) and Joe Perkins sit in the section of the bus usually reserved for whites. The deeper into the South the bus traveled, the more resistance to integration the Freedom Riders experienced. The station manager in Danville, Virginia, agreed to follow the law. But outside of Anniston, Alabama, on May 14, angry Klansmen and onlookers (seen in the reflection in the bus window), believe Southern customs, not the law, should be obeyed.

On Monday, the Freedom Riders make it to Charlotte, North Carolina. Charles Person notices his shoes need a shine, and at Union Station he takes a seat in the shoeshine chair. He isn't thinking of this as a test of the law or a challenge to local customs. He only wants his shoes shined, but he is refused service. The chair is for WHITES only. Person does not move. He stays where he is. Within minutes, a police officer arrives and threatens to handcuff him and take him to jail. Person moves to avoid arrest, but he hurries to tell the other riders what has happened.

The riders decide Joe Perkins should test the law at the shoeshine chair. It is the South's first-known

SHOE-IN.

When Perkins is told to move, he stays put. The police arrive, and he becomes the first Freedom Rider to be ARRESTED. He is charged with trespassing. Bail is set at $50. Ed Blankenheim is on hand to pay it, but Perkins chooses to remain in jail until his trial on Wednesday.

JAIL—NO BAIL.

Fill the jails. This also is part of the Freedom Riders' plan. Segregation should be so costly that cities and states, and the people they govern, realize they can no longer afford to practice discrimination.

Before Judge Howard B. Arbuckle, Perkins gets a surprise. The judge follows the law, not the Jim Crow signs of the South. The judge says Perkins is not guilty. Since his arrest, though, Perkins has had two nights' lodging, plus meals, at the expense of taxpayers.

That's part of the plan. Make it too costly to discriminate.

Perkins and Blankenheim catch a late-morning bus to Rock Hill, South Carolina. They join the other Freedom Riders there.

Al Bigelow (left) and Joe Perkins. Perkins was the first Freedom Rider to be arrested and also the first to put the jail-no-bail policy into action.

Rock Hill had been shaken by sit-ins at Woolworth's and McCrory's lunch counters throughout 1960. These were staged by students from Friendship Junior College. Many of the town's white citizens were angered that their traditions were challenged, that the signs of the South were ignored. On January 31, 1961, in the most recent round of sit-ins, a group of students were arrested and found guilty of trespassing. On February 1, they all were sentenced to either a $100 fine or thirty days of hard labor on a chain gang. For the first time in the sit-in movement, nine of those arrested chose to serve out their full sentences. Fill the jails. Make discrimination costly. The group became known as the Friendship Nine.

Now, on May 9, these same angry white citizens seethe when the Freedom Ride rolls into Rock Hill that morning. At the Greyhound terminal,

As in the Rock Hill, South Carolina, sit-ins, college students across the United States integrated previously segregated lunch counters and waited for service.

Al Bigelow and John Lewis approach the white-only waiting room. It is their legal right to enter, but two young white men in leather jackets, "a welcoming committee of hoodlums," block the way. "'Other side,'" one of them says to Lewis and points "to a door down the way with a sign that said

'COLORED.'"

Lewis tells the young man, "I have a right to go in here."

The hoodlum responds by doubling his fist and slamming it into Lewis's head. A second later he strikes again, hitting Lewis square in the face. Tasting blood, Lewis drops to the floor, as feet begin to kick him hard in the ribs.

Bigelow steps between Lewis and the men to "absorb some of the blows and kicks." He, too, is attacked and brought to his knees. The two Freedom Riders do not attempt to retaliate. They have pledged to be nonviolent like Mohandas Gandhi, leader of India's struggle to gain its independence from Great Britain.

Several other white men move to join the attack, but Genevieve Hughes steps in their way. She is knocked to the floor before a white police officer calmly tells the men, "'All right, boys. . . . Get on home.'"

When the second bus arrives later in the afternoon, the Trailways terminal and lunch counter are closed to prevent the riders from entering and carrying out their test of the law.

That night, as Lewis, Hughes, and Bigelow tell what happened, their fellow Freedom Riders begin to sense the danger of ignoring the Jim Crow signs of the South.

COLORED
WAITING ROOM
PRIVATE PROPERTY
NO PARKING
Driving through or Turning Around
BINGO
TONITE!
Good
Housekeeping
True Story
HITLER'S
LOVE LIFE
REVEALED
BY HIS
FORMER MAID
HAWAII
CAROLINA COACH

Blacks in the United States were expected to follow the Jim Crow signs of the South, even when segregation was against federal laws.

The next morning, the Freedom Riders number twelve. A bruised John Lewis is on his way to Philadelphia for a job interview with the American Friends Service Committee, a Quaker organization that promotes peace and justice throughout the world. He pledges to rejoin his friends on Monday, May 15, the day the riders are scheduled to leave Birmingham, Alabama. The remaining riders use the morning to desegregate both Rock Hill bus terminals. This time, there are no incidents, but newspapers all across the nation carry the story about the previous day's attack on Lewis, Bigelow, and Hughes. Now most of the South is aware that the Freedom Ride is on its way to New Orleans, bringing outside agitators to stir up trouble.

After the Rock Hill, South Carolina, attack, John Lewis, James Farmer (in chair), and other Freedom Riders gather to discuss what to expect as the ride goes deeper into the South.

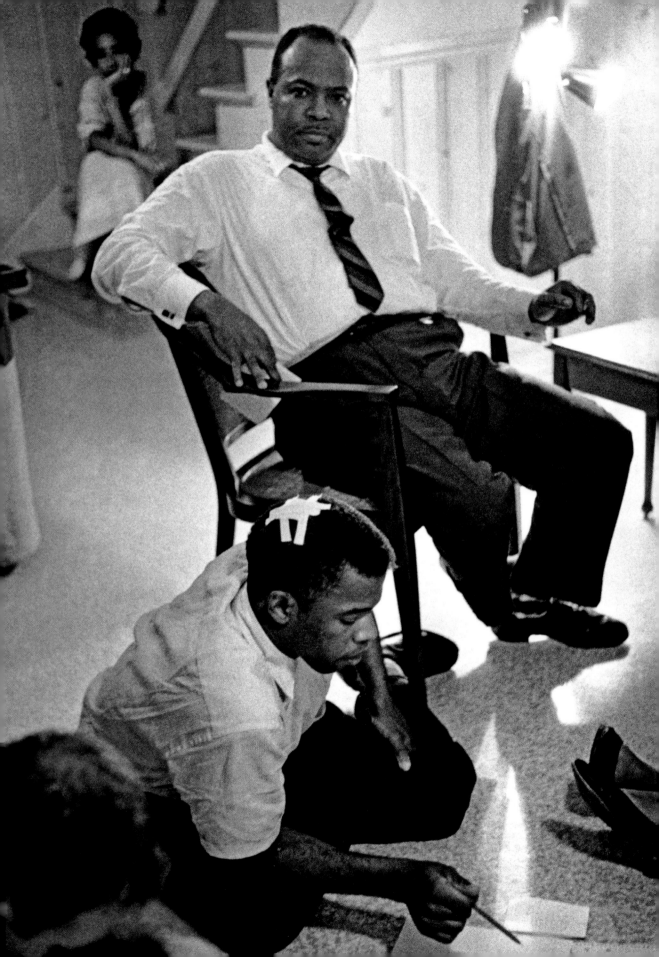

Later in the day, in Winnsboro, South Carolina, Hank Thomas sits down at the white-only lunch counter. James Peck is with him. Almost before they get settled, a brawny police officer tells Thomas to come with him. Peck explains that Thomas has a constitutional right to eat lunch wherever he wants. The officer isn't in a mood to listen. He arrests both men, Thomas on the charge of trespassing and Peck for interfering in police business.

That's the way it is in the South.

WHITE SUPREMACY. SEGREGATION. DO NOT INTERFERE IN SOUTHERN WAYS.

While Thomas and Peck sit in jail, the Freedom Ride travels on. James Farmer asks Frances Bergman to stay behind to keep an eye on the situation.

Hank Thomas was arrested and jailed for attempting to sit at a white-only lunch counter in Winnsboro, South Carolina. He was the least experienced of the original Freedom Riders with regard to protests and nonviolence. James Farmer worried that Thomas might not be able to control his temper and fists if confronted by racism.

Bergman, a retired white elementary-school teacher, later reports to Farmer that a police officer has told her to leave town. She says that as a final warning he adds, "We have no use for your kind here." Bergman ignores the order.

Later, the police drop all charges against the two Freedom Riders, but then re-arrest Peck for being in possession of a bottle of brandy that he purchased before entering the state. The bottle lacks South Carolina's required liquor-tax stamp.

Around midnight, two police officers drive Thomas to the nearly empty bus terminal, where Thomas sees several white men milling around the entrance. They look like trouble. As Thomas enters the building, one of the men orders him to the colored-only waiting room. Thomas goes into the white-only waiting room instead. He buys a candy bar and then strolls past the segregationists on his way back outside. They are stunned at being ignored, but before they can react, a car roars up and its driver orders Thomas to get inside and, expecting gunshots, to get down. Just as quickly, the car speeds away. It is driven by a local black minister whom Frances Bergman contacted earlier in the day. The minister drives Thomas to the home of an NAACP leader. The next morning, Thomas takes a bus to meet up with the other Freedom Riders in Sumter, South Carolina.

Frances and Walter Bergman were the oldest riders on Freedom Ride 1961. James Farmer asked Frances to remain in Winnsboro to look after the jailed riders because he figured that as a white woman, she probably would not experience physical harm.

Alerted by Bergman that Peck is still in jail, Farmer drives to Winnsboro in a borrowed car. Arriving just before dawn, he pays Peck's $50 bail, and Peck is released. Paying the bail is against the jail-no-bail policy, but neither Farmer nor Peck wants to wait around for Peck's day in court. Farmer ferries Peck and Bergman to Sumter, where they rejoin the other Freedom Riders.

MAY 11

On Thursday, Farmer, Peck, Thomas, and Bergman talk at a mass meeting held in Sumter's Emmanuel African Methodist Episcopal Church. Bergman brings the audience to a hushed silence as she speaks: "'For the first time I felt that I had a glimpse of what it would be like to be colored. . . . To be scorned, humiliated and made to feel like dirt.'"

In Sumter, Benjamin Cox temporarily leaves the ride in order to deliver a Mother's Day sermon at his church in High Point, North Carolina, on Sunday. James Farmer quickly finds replacements for Cox and John Lewis. Three new riders—Jerry Moore, Herman Harris, and Mae Frances Moultrie—are from Morris College, a historically black school in Sumter. A fourth black volunteer, Ike Reynolds, is from Wayne State University in Detroit, Michigan.

The Freedom Ride heads toward Atlanta on Friday, May 12. Along the way, they stop for the night in Augusta, Georgia. At the Trailways bus terminal, the signs of the South go unenforced, with one exception—a white waitress refuses to serve Joe Perkins. She makes her black co-worker serve him instead.

Large groups of students welcome the Freedom Riders with applause when they arrive in Atlanta on Saturday. Nearly all of these students are veterans of sit-ins and the civil rights movement.

They have fought for equality, following Gandhi's example of nonviolence.

The Reverend Dr. Martin Luther King, Jr., a local Baptist minister and civil rights activist, invites the riders and several of his aides to dinner that evening at one of Atlanta's most popular black-owned restaurants. King praises the riders and offers words of encouragement. The riders hope that King will join them for the remainder of the ride, but King has no intention of becoming a Freedom Rider. He tells Simeon Booker, a reporter who is traveling on the Trailways bus and covering the ride for *Jet* and *Ebony* magazines, two black-owned publications, "You will never make it through Alabama." When the waiter leaves "a large bill," James Farmer expects King to reach for the check, but to Farmer's surprise, he finds himself "picking up the tab." As the dinner breaks up, however, King shakes "hands warmly with each Freedom Rider."

Later, the riders meet for a final planning session before traveling into neighboring Alabama. At the meeting, Farmer stuns everyone by announcing that he personally will lead the desegregation tests at the Trailways bus terminals. Until now, others have tested the facilities at each stop, but he is "afraid of what lay in store for us [the riders] in Alabama." He appoints James Peck to lead the tests at the Greyhound terminals. Before going to sleep, the riders huddle and sing "We Shall Overcome."

In the middle of the night, Farmer is awakened by a telephone call from his mother. His father has died. Before the Freedom Ride began, Farmer's father had taken ill and was hospitalized. Although Farmer wants to remain with the Freedom Ride, he also is relieved "to be spared participation in it." He knows he "must return [to Washington] immediately to help bury him [his father]."

"We Don't Want No Troublemakers From The United States"

Political figures in the South accused the Freedom Riders of being outside agitators and troublemakers. But these same politicians overlooked the violence of the Ku Klux Klan and other homegrown white supremacists.

Meanwhile, in Alabama, the Ku Klux Klan is
following the progress of the Freedom Ride.
A group of white supremacists, the Klan believes
in segregation.

KEEP THE RACES APART.
KEEP THEM SEPARATE.

White here. Colored there.
The Klan has plans of its own to welcome these
outside agitators to Alabama.

MAY 14

It is Sunday—Mother's Day. James Farmer boards an Atlanta plane for Washington, D.C., to bury his father. James Peck now assumes the role of ride leader. Before leaving Atlanta, Peck telephones the Reverend Fred L. Shuttlesworth of Birmingham to tell the minister what time the Freedom Riders are scheduled to arrive in that Alabama city. Shuttlesworth, a civil rights activist, cautions Peck that the city is alive with rumors that the Klan is planning attacks at the downtown bus stations. Peck relays Shuttlesworth's warning to his fellow riders, but they all agree the ride must go on.

The Greyhound bus departs Atlanta first at 11:00 a.m. Aboard it are seven Freedom Riders: Genevieve Hughes, Al Bigelow, Hank Thomas, Jimmy McDonald, Mae Frances Moultrie, Joe Perkins, and Ed Blankenheim. Also with this group are two journalists, Charlotte Devree and Moses Newson, and two undercover officers from the Alabama Highway Patrol, Ell Cowling and Harry Sims. The riders are unaware that Cowling and Sims were sent to eavesdrop on them.

Ell Cowling was one of two white Alabama Highway Patrol undercover officers aboard the Greyhound as it journeyed into the state. When the bus was attacked, he upheld his oath to serve and to protect by blocking the door and preventing rioting Klansmen from entering.

Black and white—TOGETHER. That's the plan.

Just southeast of Anniston, Alabama, the driver of an approaching Greyhound bus waves down O. T. Jones, who is driving the Freedom Riders, and signals for him to pull over. A white man gets off the Greyhound and runs across the road. No one knows who the man is, but he tells Jones that a large, unruly crowd is gathering in Anniston. The Freedom Riders urge Jones to continue.

Minutes later, as the Greyhound crosses the city limits, the Freedom Riders notice the streets are lined with people. As the bus eases into the station parking area just after 1:00 p.m., it is eerily empty. Suddenly, a crowd of about fifty men swarm into the lot and surround the bus. They carry metal pipes, clubs, and chains. Roger Couch, a Klansman and ex-convict,

lies in front of the bus to prevent it from moving. No police are present, although earlier in the day the station manager warned them about the potential for violence. Couch's fellow Klansmen try to force their way into the bus, but the two undercover officers manage to block the door. They can do nothing to prevent the Klansmen from breaking out windows and hurling rocks and threats through them. The attack lasts for about twenty minutes before the police arrive. The police show no interest in arresting the Klansmen, but they do break up the crowd enough to clear a path for the vehicle to leave. As the bus pulls away, however, someone slashes two of its tires.

The battered Greyhound moves on toward Birmingham, Alabama. Escorted by a police vehicle, the bus is trailed by thirty to forty cars and pickup trucks full of angry, screaming white people. Many of them are dressed in their Sunday finest, having just been to church that morning. Some have their young children with them. At the town limits, the police escort turns back. The bus and its cargo of Freedom Riders are now at the mercy of the mob.

On an isolated stretch of highway about six miles southwest of Anniston, two of the trailing cars race around to the front of the bus. They slow, forcing O. T. Jones, the Greyhound driver, to reduce the speed to a crawl. The bus's slashed "left front tire" goes flat. A rear tire is worn to the metal wheel rims. Jones has no choice but to pull to the side of the road in front of Forsyth and Son, a small mom-and-pop grocery store. He throws open the door and races inside to telephone for replacement tires, but none are available. Before the crowd of unruly whites charges toward the bus, one of the undercover officers has just enough time to retrieve his weapon from the baggage area beneath the bus and reboard.

SOUTHERN WHITES ARE THE NEGROES' BEST FRIENDS BUT NO INTEGRATION

Above: **Racial hate was taught and learned at an early age.**

Right: **An unidentified bus employee, probably O. T. Jones, inspects the slashed left front tire. Without replacements for it and the rear tire, which was also slashed in Anniston, the bus was unable to carry the Freedom Riders any farther.**

The first Klansman to reach the bus is a young teen who smashes a side window with a crowbar. Other boys and men violently rock the vehicle in an attempt to overturn it as two highway patrol officers arrive on the scene. When the patrol officers make no attempt to stop the attack, the Freedom Riders and others aboard the bus decide it is safer to remain where they are. Suddenly, a burning bundle of gasoline-soaked rags stuffed into a soft-drink bottle is thrown through a broken window. It explodes in flames. The bus fills with thick, black smoke. A group of Klansmen presses against the main door, trapping the riders inside in an attempt to burn them alive.

Some of those aboard the bus drop to the ground through the broken-out windows. The two patrol officers fire their weapons into the air to warn off the mob. But an exploding fuel tank finally convinces the Klansmen to back away. The whole bus is about to go up in flames. Ell Cowling, one of the undercover officers aboard the bus, pries open the main door, and he and the remaining passengers—all choking on smoke—escape the engulfed bus and spill onto the surrounding grass. The violence does not end. Hank Thomas crawls away from the bus as a white man rushes up to him and asks if he is okay. Before Thomas can answer, the white man clubs him in the

Dazed victims, choking on smoke, spilled onto the grass at the side of the road, where some of them suffered even more violence from Klansmen carrying bats, clubs, and chains.

head with a baseball bat. Other Klansmen rush toward dazed riders lying or sitting on the grass surrounding the bus. They are driven back by the sight of Cowling's revolver and heat of the fire. A second fuel-tank explosion keeps them away.

A few nearby residents offer to help the victims. A twelve-year-old local white girl, Janie Miller, hauls five-gallon buckets of water to the riders and other passengers. Most of the local residents, however, either look on in silence or urge the Klansmen to continue their assault, until ambulances arrive to carry the injured to the hospital. At first, ambulance drivers refuse to carry any of the injured black riders. Only when the white Freedom Riders begin to crawl out of the ambulances, unwilling to leave their black friends behind, do the drivers relent and agree to carry all the victims.

At the hospital, the injured encounter more difficulties. Although doctors are coaxed into treating all the injured, not just the white riders, the hospital superintendent tells the victims they must leave as soon as they have been treated. Nightfall approaches and a crush of menacing Klansmen are threatening to burn the hospital to the ground. Joe Perkins places a frantic telephone call to the Reverend Fred Shuttlesworth to see if the minister can help.

In the South, Jim Crow affected every part of life, not just schools, buses, lunch counters, drinking fountains, and waiting rooms. Movie houses, taxis, and even hospitals and ambulances

Shuttlesworth organizes a caravan of cars from among his followers in the Alabama Christian Movement for Human Rights (ACMHR) to make their way over the region's hilly back roads to rescue the riders and return them to the safety of the minister's home in Birmingham. (The ACMHR is a local organization formed after state legislators blocked the NAACP from operating in Alabama.) The rescue mission is a dangerous one, but Shuttlesworth reminds the drivers to remain nonviolent, no matter the consequences. Even so, many of the drivers secretly carry loaded shotguns beneath their seats for protection.

Meanwhile, in Atlanta, the second bus of Freedom Riders leaves the Trailways station about an hour behind the Greyhound. Several Klansmen board the bus quietly, like ordinary passengers, along with Freedom Riders James Peck, Walter and Frances Bergman, Charles Person, Herman Harris, Jerry Moore, and Ike Reynolds. With them are Simeon Booker and *Jet* magazine photographer Ted Gaffney. As soon as the bus is underway, the Klansmen begin to verbally threaten the Freedom Riders, although they seem content for now not to do anything violent.

But the mood quickly changes as a Klansman orders Person and Harris to the back.

Blacks to the back. Whites up front.

This is the way it is in the South.

When the two riders don't move, the Klansman punches Person in the face. A second Klansman strikes Harris. When the riders don't fight back, the thugs grow more violent. They drag the two Freedom Riders into the aisle and beat them with fists. They kick them with their feet. James Peck and Walter Bergman rush forward to stop the attack, but both men are struck. Content that they have made their point, the Klansmen end their assault. They force the bloodied Freedom Riders to the back and hold them there with guns and knives as the driver steers the bus over country roads to Birmingham.

At the Birmingham Trailways station, Klansmen are ready. They are "'in the waiting room, in the rest rooms, in the parking area.'"

There are no police officers. Eugene "Bull" Connor, commissioner of the police and fire departments, supports the Klan. He has promised to delay police response by fifteen minutes in order to give the segregationists time to *welcome* the riders

A former sports broadcaster, Eugene "Bull" Connor was
first elected to public office in the 1930s and quickly gained
a reputation as an outspoken opponent of integration.
Supported by and an advocate of the Ku Klux Klan, he brought
worldwide condemnation upon Birmingham in 1963 when
he used police dogs and fire hoses against young civil rights

At 4:15 p.m., the Trailways bus rolls into the terminal. The Klansmen on the bus have done their job—enforcing Jim Crow. They run to the front, screaming a few parting taunts at the Freedom Riders before rushing out the door.

The riders collect their luggage, and James Peck and Charles Person walk toward the white-only waiting room to begin their test of the station's facilities. "I did not want to put Person in a position of being forced to proceed," writes Peck, "if he thought the situation too dangerous. When I looked at him, he responded by saying simply, 'Let's go.'"

Moments later, the two men approach the white-only lunch counter. A Klansman blocks their path and comments about the cuts on Peck's face and his blood-splattered shirt. He screams that Person should die for attacking a white man. Peck explains that Person isn't the man who attacked him. Peck says, "You'll have to kill me before you hurt him." The waiting Klansmen become more enraged. Whites do not defend blacks, no matter how innocent they may be. One Klansman physically shoves Person, saying, "The Negro waiting room is back that way." When Person steadies himself and continues to the white-only lunch counter, another segregationist shouts, "Hit him." The Klansmen begin to attack Person with their fists and feet. Peck rushes to Person's aid, but he, too, is assaulted. The two riders are pushed into a narrow passageway where more whites wait with metal pipes, and these Klansmen pounce on the men. Somehow Person breaks free. He runs into the street, boards a city bus, and finds his way to Fred Shuttlesworth's house. Peck, however, bears the brunt of the Klan attack. When it is finally over, he slumps to the floor, unconscious and lying in a pool of blood. He is found by an injured Walter Bergman. Looking like war casualties, the two eventually convince a black taxi driver to take them to Shuttlesworth's home. Here, they meet up with the other riders.

In the terminal scuffle, Ike Reynolds, who joined the ride in Sumter, South Carolina, and a couple of innocent black bystanders also are beaten and stomped on by a gang of whites. Reynolds's semiconscious body is heaved into a curbside trash bin before he and the bystanders are rescued by *CBS Evening News* reporter Howard K. Smith. Smith is in town to film a television report titled "Who Speaks for Birmingham?" The three injured blacks agree to be interviewed by Smith at Smith's motel room, but the eyewitness interview is not broadcast to CBS's national audience on the Sunday's *Evening*

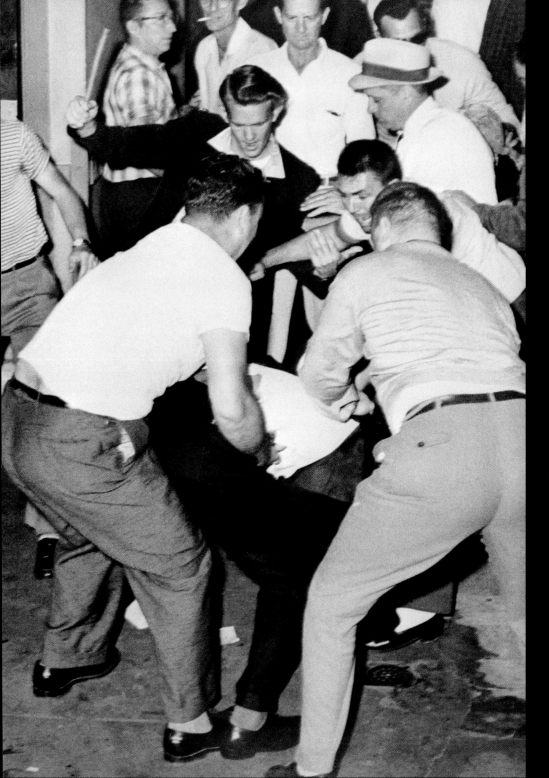

This Klan attack was originally identified as the beating of Freedom Rider James Peck at the Birmingham bus station. Years later, it was discovered that the victim actually was George Webb, a black bystander who had no hand in the Freedom Ride. The man participating with his back to the camera (right of center) was Gary Thomas Rowe, an FBI undercover agent.

can't get a signal, but Smith suspects the problem
has more to do with the station owner's support of
Jim Crow.

By the time the police arrive, the Klansmen are
gone. They have had the fifteen minutes Connor
promised them.

With the Freedom Riders now all gathered at the
Shuttlesworth house, the police and Bull Connor
threaten to arrest and jail everyone. The minister and
the riders are violating Birmingham's strict housing
segregation law. In Birmingham, blacks and whites
do not live under the same roof.

White here. Colored there.

KEEP THE RACES APART. KEEP THEM SEPARATE.

Shuttlesworth doesn't back down. He tells the
commissioner the riders are staying where they
are. Connor does nothing, but he fumes that
Shuttlesworth isn't intimidated.

The minister is especially worried about James
Peck, who is drifting in and out of consciousness.
Shuttlesworth arranges for an ambulance to take
Peck to Carraway Methodist Hospital, but doctors

James Peck and Jimmy McDonald (right). Peck's bandages were the result of the Klan attack at the Birmingham Trailways station.

gathered, and he vows to return to the Freedom Ride on Monday.

MAY 15

Day 12, Monday. News media throughout the nation, and the world, carry reports of the Freedom Ride attacks outside Anniston and in Birmingham. No one outside the South can understand the violence. People worldwide are shocked and dismayed.

James Farmer is following the situation from Washington, D.C. He decides the ride is too risky to continue, but a majority of Freedom Riders in Shuttlesworth's living room overrule him. They vote to continue the ride. Getting out of Birmingham, however, is a problem. Scheduled buses to Montgomery either are canceled or bus drivers are unwilling to transport the Freedom Riders. With no buses available to them, they decide late in the afternoon to fly to New Orleans.

At the airport, they run into more obstacles. An anonymous bomb threat forces the cancellation of their first flight. More bomb scares scrap two later flights as well. By this time, it is past eight o'clock. Finally, John Seigenthaler, a Southerner and a representative of the U.S. Department of Justice (DOJ) who is at the airport trying to negotiate the riders' departure, instructs the airport manager to sneak the Freedom Riders on a plane, announce the flight, and then under no circumstances answer the phone. The DOJ representative has been sent by the administration of President John F. Kennedy to try to gain control of the situation. Seigenthaler knows that as soon as the flight is announced, it will cause more bomb threats and another cancellation.

At 10:38 p.m., a Capital Airlines plane rumbles down the runway and lifts skyward. The Freedom Riders are finally on their way out of Birmingham.

About one hour later, the plane lands in New Orleans. After the events in Birmingham, the Freedom Riders are surprised to be given a hero's welcome by local civil rights activists and others who also are in the city to commemorate the *Brown* decision.

Freedom Ride 1961 is over. Battered and bruised, the Freedom Riders have met their goal of arriving in New Orleans by May 17. They have shown the

On May 17, 1961, just days after being beaten in Alabama, James Peck (right) and Hank Thomas (left) stand on a protest line at the Trailways bus station in New York City's Port Authority Bus Terminal.

country and the world that in some parts of the United States black Americans are treated as second-class citizens, that laws are not enforced equally and with an even hand throughout the land. Their brave journey, and the acts of others who follow, eventually lead President John F. Kennedy to urge fairness and equality for all Americans. He asks the U.S. Congress to take action on legislation. On July 2, 1964, President Lyndon B. Johnson signs the Civil Rights Act into law, so that America can live up to its promise "that all . . . are created equal."

BEYOND
BIRMINGHAM

The first official Freedom Ride, the Journey of
Reconciliation of 1947, was an attempt to challenge
those states that did not recognize the U.S.
Supreme Court's decision in *Morgan v. Commonwealth
of Virginia* (1946). This decision ruled that
segregated seating on public transportation created
a hardship on bus companies doing interstate
business. This ruling made it illegal to require
blacks to sit in the back of the bus if it crossed
state boundaries. At a time when segregated
seating was commonplace throughout the South and
accepted by most blacks as something they must put
up with, the Congress of Racial Equality (CORE)

looked for a way to highlight the division between law and what was really happening. CORE's parent organization, a pacifist group called the Fellowship of Reconciliation (FOR), agreed. The idea of a peaceful, interracial bus ride was born—the Journey of Reconciliation. But as the 1940s drew to a close, it was clear that the goal of eliminating segregation had not been fulfilled.

When James Farmer, a founding member of CORE, was asked to lead the organization in 1961, he decided the time was right for another ride based on the original Journey of Reconciliation. The 1960 Supreme Court decision in *Boynton v. Virginia* ruled that interstate travel facilities—waiting rooms, restaurants, and restrooms—were for the use of everyone, regardless of race, and should not be segregated. Farmer organized Freedom Ride 1961 to draw attention to the fact that laws still were not being followed and that people, on the basis of their skin color, were being treated as second-class citizens.

When the ride couldn't continue as planned, college students from nearby Nashville, Tennessee, swarmed to Birmingham. Farmer writes in *Lay Bare the Heart: An Autobiography of the Civil Rights Movement*: "I got a call at home from Diane Nash,

Diane Nash, a Fisk University student in Nashville, Tennessee, was active in the Nashville Student Movement and the Student Nonviolent Coordinating Committee. When violence seemed to stop the Freedom Ride in Birmingham, she worked with James Farmer and the Congress of Racial Equality so it might continue.

a leader of the Student Non-Violent Coordinating Committee (SNCC) in Nashville, Tennessee. [The Student Nonviolent Coordinating Committee was inspired by the sit-ins in Greensboro and Nashville to fight segregation at public libraries, community swimming pools, movie theaters, and lunch counters.] In line with the unwritten pact between CORE and SNCC that neither organization would move in on the other's project without permission, Diane said to me, 'Your group of Freedom Riders are so badly chewed up that they cannot go on now. Would you have any objections to members of the Nashville Student Movement, which is SNCC, going in and taking up the Ride where CORE left off?'

"'You realize it may be suicide,' I replied.

"'We fully realize that,' she said, . . . 'but we can't let them stop us with violence. If we do, the movement is dead.'"

The Freedom Rides continued under the combined leadership of SNCC and CORE throughout 1961. Riders came from all parts of the United States—men and women, young and old, black and white—in all, some 436 Freedom Riders. They had a plan; they were people with the dream of equality.

Under the joint direction of the Congress of Racial Equality and the Student Nonviolent Coordinating Committee, students from Nashville, Tennessee, continue the ride from Birmingham to Montgomery, Alabama's state capital, on Saturday, May 20, 1961. In response to unchecked mob violence that greets the Freedom Riders, the governor eventually calls out the National Guard to give them safe passage.

The Reverend Fred L. Shuttlesworth speaks with students who arrived in Birmingham to continue the Freedom Ride. Shuttlesworth, a civil rights activist, led the fight for black equality in that city from the early 1950s. He joined the Freedom Ride on May 24, when he rode from Atlanta to Montgomery. The next day, before boarding the bus headed to Jackson, Mississippi, he was arrested for requesting service at the Montgomery station's white-only lunch counter.

Levert Taylor (second from right) and Glenda Jackson were arrested by Officer W. L. Copeland in Jackson, Mississippi, in a November 1961 wave of Freedom Riders. They were charged with disturbing the peace for refusing to leave the white waiting room at the bus station.

THE THIRTEEN
FREEDOM
RIDERS

James Farmer

A founding member of CORE, a racially mixed group
dedicated to nonviolence and ending segregation,
Farmer became its national director in February 1961.
Immediately, he set about organizing the ride and
interviewing participants to make sure they could
follow the Gandhian discipline of nonviolence. He
took part in the ride from Washington, D.C., to Atlanta,
Georgia. Awarded the Presidential Medal of Freedom
in 1998 by President Bill Clinton, he died the
next year.

James Peck

Peck was a conscientious objector during World War II and an antiwar, antinuclear activist. He was the only rider to participate in the Journey of Reconciliation (1947) and the Freedom Ride (1961). He passed away in 1993.

Genevieve Hughes

Hughes grew up in the upper-middle-class suburban community of Chevy Chase, Maryland. She became active in CORE after she moved to New York City to work as a stockbroker, and she eventually joined the organization as a field secretary. John Lewis described her as being "as graceful and gentle as her name," and "not at all afraid to speak up when she had strong feelings about something." She continued to be active in social justice and environmental issues until her death in 2012.

Joseph "Joe" P. Perkins Jr.

Perkins was a field secretary with CORE in 1961. Originally from Owensboro, Kentucky, he studied at Kentucky State University in Frankfort before enlisting in the army in 1954, where he served two years as a medical technician. Later, he studied music at Howard University before transferring to the University of Michigan, where he became active in the Ann Arbor Direct Action Committee. He died in 1976.

Plumes of thick, black smoke billow from the Greyhound bus
on Mother's Day, May 14, 1961.

Walter and Frances Bergman

The Bergmans were from Michigan, where Walter was a leading figure in the teachers' union movement of the 1930s and 1940s, serving as president of the Michigan Federation of Teachers. A part-time professor at the University of Michigan and Wayne State University, he was confined to a wheelchair after the Freedom Ride as a result of the beating he received aboard the Birmingham-bound Trailways bus. He continued to fight for social justice until his death in 1999 at age one hundred.

Frances, Walter's wife, died in 1979 at the age of seventy-five. Like her husband, she remained active in social justice issues until her death.

Albert Smith Bigelow

The son of a Harvard-educated lawyer, Bigelow became a devout Quaker and pacifist after the United States dropped atomic bombs on Hiroshima and Nagasaki in World War II. He gained an international reputation in 1958 after he captained the Golden Rule, a sailing yacht, into a nuclear drop zone in the Pacific Ocean to protest America's scheduled testing of nuclear weapons. He died in 1993.

Ed Blankenheim (kneeling) and Hank Thomas (with back to camera) douse their eyes with water brought to them by Janie Miller on May 14. Ridiculed, snubbed, and threatened by neighbors for her act of kindness, Miller and her family are forced to move out of Anniston.

Jimmy McDonald

McDonald participated in a number of CORE-sponsored direct-action campaigns, but James Farmer considered him to be the least reliable rider because he wasn't committed to Gandhi's nonviolent philosophy. McDonald said the only reason he was allowed to join the Freedom Ride was because he knew a lot of labor and freedom songs. He died in 2000 at the age of sixty-nine.

Edward "Ed" Blankenheim

Originally from Minnesota and raised in Illinois, Blankenheim was a member of Tucson's NAACP Youth Council and a leader in a local CORE chapter. The father of two left Tucson to join the ride in Washington, D.C. He was arrested in 2000 while advocating for handicapped bus riders and died in San Francisco in 2004 at the age of seventy.

Henry "Hank" Thomas

Thomas was a native of rural Florida and one of eleven children in an impoverished family with an abusive father. He was well prepared for the ride, having grown up in the South. He also had attended the founding conference of SNCC in April 1960. He served as a medic in the Vietnam War in 1965 and was awarded the Purple

Recovered luggage sits beside the road as firefighters attempt to extinguish the blaze on May 14.

Heart for wounds he received in that conflict. Today,
he is a civic leader and businessman in Atlanta,
Georgia, where he lives with his wife.

Charles Person

A Georgia native, Person was a member of the local
NAACP Youth Council. He earned a sixteen-day jail
sentence for his participation in an Atlanta sit-in.
Still a minor at the time of the ride, he had to talk
his father into signing a CORE permission form before
being allowed to join. (His mother refused to sign.)
After Freedom Ride 1961, he went on to a twenty-
year career in the Marine Corps and later ran his own
electronics company. In the 1980s, after retiring, he
returned to Atlanta, where he volunteers as a tutor
and mentor for high-school students.

Benjamin Elton Cox

NAACP leaders wanted at least one ordained minister
on the Freedom Ride and suggested Cox to James Farmer.
Cox readily agreed to participate in the ride. In
December 1961, he was arrested in Baton Rouge,
Louisiana, on charges of disturbing the peace, blocking
public passages, and picketing before a courthouse when
he led students from Southern University on a peaceful

All that remained of the Greyhound after the attack was a shell. Here, a firefighter searches through the debris in the days immediately following the Mother's Day assault on May 14.

march to protest segregation. Despite having stopped the march one hundred feet from the courthouse, he was convicted on all three charges. In a case known as *Cox v. Louisiana*, his convictions were overturned in 1965 by the U.S. Supreme Court. He left CORE that same year but continued to fight for civil rights throughout his life. He died at age seventy-nine in 2011.

John Lewis

Born in Alabama, Lewis was the first in his family to go to college. He enrolled in the American Baptist Theological Seminary in Nashville, Tennessee. He quickly became involved in the Nashville Student Movement and was arrested during a 1960 sit-in. On his application to become a Freedom Rider, he wrote, "At this time, human dignity is the most important thing in my life. This is the most important decision in my life, to decide to give up all if necessary for the Freedom Ride, that Justice and Freedom might come to the Deep South." Although he left the Freedom Ride after the Rock Hill incident, he returned to it with the Nashville students when SNCC took up the ride. He has represented Georgia's Fifth Congressional District since 1987.

BIBLIOGRAPHY

SOURCES CONSULTED BY THE AUTHOR

Arsenault, Raymond. *Freedom Riders: 1961 and the Struggle for Racial Justice.*
New York: Oxford University Press, 2006.

Farmer, James. *Lay Bare the Heart: An Autobiography of the Civil Rights
Movement.* Fort Worth: Texas Christian University Press, 1998.

Kaufman, Dorothy B. *The First Freedom Ride: The Walter Bergman Story.*
Detroit: ACLU Fund Press, 1989.

Lewis, John. *Walking with the Wind: A Memoir of the Movement.* With Michael
D'Orso. New York: Simon and Schuster, 1998.

Peck, James. *Freedom Ride.* New York: Grove Press, 1962.

Assorted newspaper articles, including those from the *Anniston* (AL) *Star,* the
Augusta (GA) *Chronicle,* the *Bridgeport* (CT) *Telegram,* the *Lebanon* (PA)
Daily News, the *Evening Herald* (Rock Hill, SC), the *Independent* (Long
Beach, CA), the *New York Times,* the *San Bernardino* (CA) *Sun,* and the
Washington Post.

VIDEO

Eyes on the Prize. Blackside, Inc., for American Experience/PBS, 1986.

Freedom Riders: Threatened. Attacked. Jailed. A Stanley Nelson film/Firelight Media Production for American Experience/PBS, 2011.

WEBSITES*

BlackPast.org.
  blackpast.org/aah/freedom-rides-1961

CORE: Congress of Racial Equality.
  core-online.org/History/freedom%20rides.htm

"Equal Access to Public Accommodations." Virginia Historical Society.
  vahistorical.org/collections-and-resources/virginia-history-explorer/civil-
  rights-movement-virginia/equal-access

"Freedom Rides." History.com.
  history.com/topics/black-history/freedom-rides

"Get on the Bus: The Freedom Riders of 1961." NPR.
  npr.org/2006/01/12/5149667/get-on-the-bus-the-freedom-riders-of-1961

FOR YOUNGER READERS

Aretha, David. *The Story of the Civil Rights Freedom Rides in Photographs*. Berkeley Heights, NJ: Enslow Publishing, 2014.

Bausum, Ann. *Freedom Riders: John Lewis and Jim Zwerg on the Front Lines of the Civil Rights Movement*. Washington, DC: National Geographic Children's Books, 2006.

Brimner, Larry Dane. *Birmingham Sunday*. Honesdale, PA: Calkins Creek, 2010.

Websites active at time of publication

————. *Black & White: The Confrontation between Reverend Fred L. Shuttlesworth and Eugene "Bull" Connor.* Honesdale, PA: Calkins Creek, 2011.

————. *We Are One: The Story of Bayard Rustin.* Honesdale, PA: Calkins Creek, 2007.

Haskins, James. *Freedom Rides: Journey for Justice.* East Orange, NJ: Just Us Books, 2005 (paperback edition).

Krull, Kathleen. *What Was the March on Washington?* Illustrated by Tim Tomkinson. New York: Grosset and Dunlap, 2013.

Pinkney, Andrea Davis. *Sit-In: How Four Friends Stood Up by Sitting Down.* Illustrated by Brian Pinkney. New York: Little, Brown, 2010.

PLACES TO VISIT

Freedom Riders National Monument in Anniston, Alabama, is new and in progress. The park includes the former Anniston Greyhound Bus Station at 1031 Gurnee Avenue and the bus burning site outside of town. An Alabama Historical Marker identifies the site. A self-guided driving tour is provided at https://www.nps.gov/frri/index.htm.

ACKNOWLEDGMENTS

I extend a heartfelt thanks to the following: Laura Anderson, archivist, Birmingham Civil Rights Institute; Joan Browning, expert reader (myweb. wvnet.edu/~oma00013/); James L. Baggett, archivist, Birmingham Public Library, Department of Archives and Manuscripts; Susan Smith, reference librarian, Sumter County Library, Sumter, South Carolina; Tim L. Pennycuff, university archivist and associate professor, University of Alabama at Birmingham; and Mary Mallaney, reference librarian, York County Library, Rock Hill, South Carolina. Special thanks to librarian Cindy Clevenger, who asked for a book about the Freedom Ride aimed at younger readers, and to Kathleen Krull, for passing the idea along to me. I hope I have done justice to the topic.

Firefighter Enoch Hughes retrieves a camera from the burned Greyhound when inspecting the bus after the May 14 blaze near Anniston was put out. In the Birmingham Trailways attack that Mother's Day, *Jet* magazine photographer Ted Gaffney lost his camera and much of his film.

SOURCE NOTES

page 18
"bag containing . . .": Arsenault, p. 112.

"one by . . .": Lewis, p. 135.

"Freedom Ride 1961": "Pilgrimage Off on Racial Test," by Elsie Carper,
 Washington Post, May 5, 1961, p. B4.

page 23
"sit-in on . . .": "Mobile Sit-In Group Due in RH Today," *Evening Herald*
 (Rock Hill, SC), May 9, 1961, p. 2.

page 24
"a few cold . . .": Lewis, p. 136.

page 25

"It's a beautiful . . .": Alan B. Shepard, "U.S. Hurls Man 115 Miles into Space; Shepard Works Controls in Capsule, Reports by Radio in 15-Minute Flight," by Richard Witkin, *New York Times*, May 6, 1961.

page 28

"If God had . . .": Unidentified preacher, quoted in Arsenault, p. 117.

page 38

"a welcoming committee . . .": Unidentified speaker, quoted in "Bi-Racial Tourists Tell of Scuffle at Bus Station," *Evening Herald* (Rock Hill, SC), May 10, 1961, p. 2.

"'Other side'": Unidentified speaker, quoted in Lewis, p. 137.

"to a door . . .": Lewis, Ibid.

"I have a . . .": Lewis, Ibid.

"absorb some . . .": Al Bigelow, quoted in "'Peace Corps' Trio Charges Beating by 'White Hoodlums'," *Anniston* (AL) *Star*, May 10, 1961, p. 2.

"'All right, boys . . .'": Unidentified police officer, quoted in Lewis, p. 138.

page 46

"We have no . . .": Unidentified police officer, quoted in Arsenault, p. 125.

page 48

"'For the first . . .'": Frances Bergman, quoted in Arsenault, p. 128.

page 50–51

"You will never . . .": Martin Luther King, Jr., quoted in Lewis, p. 140.

"a large bill" and "picking up the tab." and "hands warmly . . .": Farmer, p. 200.

page 51
"afraid of . . ." and "to be spared . . ." and "must return . . .": Ibid, p. 201.

page 61
"left front tire": Joseph Perkins, quoted in "Negro Group Bombed in Racial Test," *Independent* (Long Beach, CA), May 15, 1961, p. 1.

page 70
"'in the waiting . . .'": Gary Thomas Rowe, quoted in Arsenault, p. 153.

page 72
"I did not . . .": Peck, p. 98.

"You'll have to . . .": Peck, quoted in Arsenault, p. 155.

"The Negro waiting . . .": Unidentified man, quoted in "Whites Ambush 'Freedom Rider' Buses in Dixie," *Bridgeport* (CT) *Telegram*, May 15, 1961, p. 4.

"Hit him.": Unidentified men, quoted in Ibid.

page 82
"I got a call . . .": Farmer, p. 203.

page 89
"as graceful . . ." and "not at all . . .": Lewis, p. 134.

page 97
"At this time . . .": Ibid, p. 129.

INDEX

Page numbers in **boldface** refer to images and/or captions.

PICTURE CREDITS

MORE CIVIL RIGHTS TITLES BY
LARRY DANE BRIMNER
FROM CALKINS CREEK

Black & White: The Confrontation between Reverend Fred L. Shuttlesworth and Eugene "Bull" Connor

Sibert Honor Book
Carter G. Woodson Book Award
ALSC Notable Children's Book
Norman A. Sugarman Children's Biography Honor Award
Booklist Top 10 Black History Book for Youth
Notable Books for a Global Society Book Award
A Chicago Public Library Best of the Best Book
A *Kirkus Reviews* Best Children's Book

Birmingham Sunday

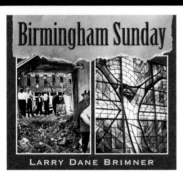

Orbis Pictus Award Honor Book
A *Kirkus Reviews* Best Children's Book
Jane Addams Honor Book for Older Children

We Are One: The Story of Bayard Rustin

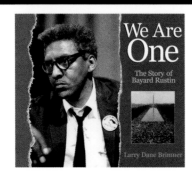

Jane Addams Book Award for Older Children
Norman A. Sugarman Children's Biography Award
New York Public Library Books for the Teen Age